Introduction

In today's fast-paced and demanding world, the ability to multitask effectively has become a valuable skill. Whether you're a student juggling multiple assignments, a professional handling various projects, or a parent managing household responsibilities, mastering the art of multitasking can significantly enhance productivity and help you unlock your full potential. This book explores the science, strategies, and benefits of multitasking, providing practical tips to harness its power and excel in all areas of life and provides a step-by-step guide on how to cultivate effective multitasking skills. Readers will learn practical techniques to improve focus, prioritize tasks, and maintain clarity amid the myriad of responsibilities that characterize modern life. The book also emphasizes the importance of adaptability and self-awareness, helping readers recognize their individual multitasking strengths and weaknesses.
Beyond personal development, "The Power of Multitasking" delves into its impact on teamwork and collaboration. Drawing from successful case studies and experiences of high-performing organizations, the book demonstrates how synchronized multitasking can lead to enhanced project management, problem-solving, and seamless coordination among team members.

Table of Contents: The Power of Multitasking

Chapter 1: Understanding Multitasking

In this chapter, we will delve into the concept of multitasking, exploring what it means and how it affects our brain's cognitive functions. We will uncover the truth behind multitasking myths and address common misconceptions, helping you build a solid foundation for embracing its power.

Chapter 2: The Science of Multitasking

This chapter delves into the neurological aspects of multitasking. Understanding how our brain handles multiple tasks simultaneously is vital to improving our multitasking abilities. We will explore studies and research that shed light on the brain's capacity for handling multiple tasks, as well as its limitations. By comprehending the brain's capabilities and limitations, we can fine-tune our multitasking strategies for maximum efficiency.

Chapter 3: The Benefits of Multitasking

Multitasking isn't just a convenient way to handle numerous tasks; it also offers a range of benefits. In this chapter, we will explore how multitasking can enhance productivity, time management, and creativity. We will also discuss its role in stress reduction and its potential to improve decision-making skills.

Chapter 4: Multitasking Techniques

This chapter is dedicated to various multitasking techniques that can be applied in different scenarios. We will cover strategies for managing work, studies, personal life, and more. From time-blocking and task prioritization to multitasking tools and technologies, you will learn how to optimize your efforts without feeling overwhelmed.

Chapter 5: Overcoming Multitasking Challenges

While multitasking can be a powerful tool, it also comes with its share of challenges. In this chapter, we will address common obstacles and furnish strategies to overcome them. We will discuss methods to maintain focus, avoid distractions, and prevent burnout, ensuring that your multitasking endeavors are successful and sustainable.

Chapter 6: Finding Balance

Amidst the hustle and bustle of multitasking, it's crucial to find balance in life. This chapter emphasizes the importance of self-care, time for relaxation, and setting realistic expectations. You'll discover how to strike a healthy equilibrium between productivity and personal well-being.

Chapter 7: Multitasking for Personal Development

Multitasking isn't limited to professional or academic pursuits; it can also be an excellent tool for personal development. In this chapter, we explore how to use multitasking to pursue hobbies, learn new skills, and broaden your horizons, fostering personal growth and fulfillment.

Chapter 8: Multitasking and Relationships

Multitasking can impact our relationships positively or negatively, depending on how we manage it. This chapter analyzes the role of multitasking in various relationships, offering insights into effective communication, active listening, and meaningful connections.

Chapter 9: Navigating the Digital Age

In today's digital age, multitasking often involves managing numerous devices and online platforms. This chapter guides handling digital distractions, striking a balance between virtual and real-world interactions, and ensuring online safety and privacy.

Conclusion

In the final chapter, we recap the power of multitasking and its potential to unlock your full potential. By applying the knowledge gained from this book, you can become a more efficient multitasker, optimize your productivity, and achieve greater success in all aspects of life. Embrace the art of multitasking, and watch as your abilities soar to new heights.

Chapter 10: Multitasking for Entrepreneurs

In this chapter, we explore how multitasking plays a crucial role in the entrepreneurial journey. From managing a startup to handling marketing, finances, and team collaboration, entrepreneurs can benefit from effective multitasking techniques to boost productivity and drive success.

Chapter 11: Multitasking and Time Management

Time management is a key component of successful multitasking. This chapter delves deeper into time management strategies, including the Pomodoro Technique, time-blocking methods, and creating efficient routines to maximize productivity.

Chapter 12: Multitasking and Creativity

Discover how multitasking can foster creativity and innovation. We explore how engaging in diverse tasks simultaneously can facilitate your mind, enhance problem-solving abilities, and lead to groundbreaking ideas.

Chapter 13: Multitasking in a Remote Work Environment

With the rise of remote work, multitasking has evolved even more crucial. This chapter provides insights into multitasking while working from home, managing virtual teams, and maintaining work-life balance in a remote setting.

Chapter 14: Multitasking and Learning

Explore the connection between multitasking and knowing. We discuss multitasking techniques to enhance learning efficiency, such as combining reading with listening or incorporating visuals into study materials.

Chapter 15: Multitasking and Health

This chapter focuses on the impact of multitasking on physical and mental health. We address potential health risks and provide strategies to mitigate stress and maintain well-being while multitasking.

Chapter 16: Multitasking in High-Pressure Situations

In challenging situations, multitasking skills become even more critical. This chapter offers guidance on staying calm under pressure, making quick decisions, and managing multiple responsibilities during demanding times.

Chapter 17: Multitasking and Continuous Improvement

Learn how to use multitasking as a tool for continuous improvement. We explore the concept of Kaizen, encouraging small incremental changes to achieve significant progress in various aspects of life.

Chapter 18: Multitasking for Busy Parents

For parents juggling numerous roles, multitasking is a lifesaver. This chapter provides practical tips for parents to multitask effectively, balancing family responsibilities, work, and personal growth.

Chapter 19: Multitasking and Emotional Intelligence

Understanding emotions while multitasking is vital for personal and professional relationships. We explore how emotional intelligence plays a role in multitasking and how to manage emotions effectively during simultaneous tasks.

Chapter 20: Multitasking and Decision-Making

Multitasking can influence decision-making processes. This chapter discusses multitasking's effects on decision quality and how to optimize decision-making while handling multiple tasks.

Chapter 21: Multitasking and Goal Setting

Learn how multitasking can be aligned with goal setting to achieve long-term objectives. We explore setting SMART goals and incorporating multitasking strategies to accomplish them efficiently.

Chapter 22: Multitasking and Public Speaking

Incorporate multitasking techniques into public speaking engagements to improve performance and engage the audience effectively. This chapter provides tips for multitasking while maintaining composure and delivering compelling speeches.

Chapter 23: Multitasking for Students

For students managing classes, assignments, and extracurricular activities, multitasking skills are indispensable. This chapter offers multitasking approaches tailored to students' needs, helping them excel academically and beyond.

Chapter 24: Multitasking and Negotiation

Effective multitasking can enhance negotiation skills. We explore how multitasking can aid in assessing various aspects of negotiations and making strategic decisions during the process.

Chapter 25: Multitasking and Networking

Networking events often involve managing multiple conversations and tasks simultaneously. This chapter provides tips for multitasking during networking events to build meaningful connections and expand your professional network.

Chapter 26: Multitasking and Traveling

Traveling involves multitasking to navigate new environments, manage schedules, and experience new cultures. This chapter offers insights into multitasking while traveling to make the most of your adventures.

Chapter 27: Multitasking and Technology

Explore the relationship between multitasking and technology, including the pros and cons of using technology as a multitasking aid and strategies to avoid digital overload.

Chapter 28: Multitasking and Volunteering

For those engaged in volunteering activities, multitasking skills can be invaluable. This chapter discusses how multitasking can aid in managing volunteer responsibilities and making a meaningful impact in the community.

Chapter 29: Multitasking and Financial Management

Efficient multitasking can positively impact personal finance management. We explore how multitasking techniques can be applied to budgeting, investing, and achieving financial goals.

Chapter 30: Multitasking and Project Management

Project managers often handle various tasks simultaneously. This chapter provides multitasking strategies specific to project management, ensuring successful project completion and team coordination.

Chapter 31: Multitasking and Workplace Collaboration

Discover how multitasking can improve workplace collaboration, communication, and teamwork. We explore multitasking techniques for a harmonious and productive work environment.

Chapter 32: Multitasking and Continuous Learning

Embrace multitasking as a means to foster continuous learning and professional growth. This chapter discusses how to multitask effectively while attending workshops, webinars, or pursuing certifications.

Chapter 33: Multitasking and Crisis Management

In times of crisis, multitasking can be a critical asset. This chapter provides insights into multitasking during crisis management, enabling quick responses and effective problem-solving.

Chapter 34: Multitasking and Language Learning

For language enthusiasts, multitasking can aid in language learning endeavors. We discuss how to combine language learning with other tasks to optimize language acquisition.

Chapter 35: Multitasking and Social Media Management

Managing a social media presence can be overwhelming without multitasking skills. This chapter offers strategies for multitasking while handling social media marketing and engagement.

Chapter 36: Multitasking and Adaptability

Adaptability is essential in a dynamic world. We explore how multitasking can enhance adaptability and help individuals thrive in ever-changing environments.

Chapter 37: Multitasking and Entrepreneurial Networking

For entrepreneurs, networking is crucial. This chapter delves into multitasking during networking events, conferences, and meetings, fostering valuable connections for business growth.

Chapter 38: Multitasking and Mindfulness

Contrary to popular belief, multitasking can coexist with mindfulness. This chapter discusses how to blend multitasking with mindfulness techniques for a balanced and focused approach.

Chapter 39: Multitasking and Conflict Resolution

Multitasking skills can be beneficial in resolving conflicts effectively. This chapter explores how to handle multiple aspects of conflicts simultaneously, leading to more satisfactory resolutions.

Chapter 40: Multitasking and Public Relations

Public relations professionals can utilize multitasking to manage media relations, crisis communications, and brand reputation. This chapter offers tips for multitasking in the PR field.

Chapter 41: Multitasking and Physical Fitness

Discover how multitasking can enhance physical fitness routines. We explore ways to incorporate multitasking into exercise and other health-related activities for a holistic approach to well-being.

Chapter 42: Multitasking and Project-Based Learning

Incorporate multitasking techniques into project-based learning for students and educators alike. This chapter provides strategies for multitasking during project creation, collaboration, and presentation.

Chapter 43: Multitasking and Career Advancement

Multitasking can be a catalyst for career growth. We explore how to leverage multitasking skills to handle additional responsibilities, seek new opportunities, and advance professionally.

Chapter 44: Multitasking and Organizational Skills

Organizational skills are closely linked to multitasking abilities. This chapter offers insights into multitasking and organization, ensuring efficient task management.

Chapter 45: Multitasking and Cybersecurity

Learn how multitasking can play a role in enhancing cybersecurity practices. We explore how to manage multiple security tasks simultaneously, protecting personal and professional data.

Chapter 46: Multitasking and Event Planning

Event planners often juggle various tasks at once. This chapter offers multitasking strategies specific to event planning, ensuring successful and memorable events.

Chapter 47: Multitasking and Sales

In the sales industry, multitasking is essential for managing leads, follow-ups, and closing deals. This chapter discusses how multitasking can lead to increased sales performance.

Chapter 48: Multitasking and Conflict Management

Multitasking skills are valuable when handling conflicts in various settings. We explore how to navigate multiple conflict management tasks while maintaining empathy and objectivity.

Chapter 49: Multitasking and Personal Branding

Discover how multitasking can boost personal branding efforts. This chapter discusses how to manage social media presence, content creation, and networking for personal branding success.

Chapter 50: Multitasking and Remote Learning

As remote learning becomes more prevalent, mastering multitasking is crucial for students and educators. This chapter offers strategies to multitask effectively in virtual learning environments.

Chapter 51: Multitasking and Cross-Functional Teams

Cross-functional teams require effective multitasking and collaboration. This chapter explores how to multitask while working with colleagues from diverse backgrounds and areas of expertise.

Chapter 52: Multitasking and Work-Life Integration

Achieving work-life integration requires adept multitasking skills. We discuss how to balance professional and personal responsibilities while avoiding burnout.

Chapter 53: Multitasking and Crisis Communication

During crises, multitasking can be pivotal in managing communication efforts. This chapter offers strategies to multitask while handling crisis communication and public relations.

Chapter 54: Multitasking and Digital Marketing

Digital marketers often manage multiple campaigns and platforms simultaneously. This chapter discusses how multitasking can optimize digital marketing efforts and drive results.

Chapter 55: Multitasking and Environmental Awareness

Multitasking can be applied to environmental initiatives and sustainability efforts. We explore how to combine multiple eco-friendly activities for a positive impact on the planet.

Chapter 56: Multitasking and Decision Fatigue

Prolonged multitasking can lead to decision fatigue. This chapter provides insights into managing decision-making while multitasking and preventing decision-making burnout.

Chapter 57: Multitasking and Corporate Social Responsibility

Embrace multitasking to advance corporate social responsibility initiatives. This chapter discusses how to manage multiple CSR projects and community engagement activities effectively.

Chapter 58: Multitasking and Language Translation

Multitasking can aid in language translation and interpretation services. We explore how to handle multiple language tasks while maintaining accuracy and efficiency.

Chapter 59: Multitasking and Crisis Leadership

During crises, leaders must multitask effectively to navigate challenges. This chapter provides guidance on multitasking during crisis leadership and decision-making.

Chapter 60: Multitasking and Continuous Assessment

Discover how multitasking can enhance continuous assessment in educational and professional settings. We explore methods to manage ongoing assessments while handling other responsibilities.

Chapter 61: Multitasking and Learning Disabilities

For individuals with learning disabilities, multitasking can present unique challenges. This chapter discusses strategies to support multitasking and learning in such cases.

Chapter 62: Multitasking and Social Entrepreneurship

Social entrepreneurs can leverage multitasking to manage business operations and social impact initiatives simultaneously. This chapter provides tips for multitasking in the realm of social entrepreneurship.

Chapter 63: Multitasking and Aging Brain

As we age, multitasking abilities may change. This chapter explores how to maintain and improve multitasking skills in older adulthood.

Chapter 64: Multitasking and Conflict Negotiation

Negotiators must handle various aspects of conflict resolution simultaneously. This chapter discusses multitasking strategies for successful conflict negotiation.

Chapter 65: Multitasking and Remote Team Management

Remote team managers face unique multitasking challenges. This chapter offers insights into multitasking while leading virtual teams effectively.

Chapter 66: Multitasking and Cybersecurity Awareness

Individuals can multitask to improve their cybersecurity awareness and protect against cyber threats. This chapter discusses multitasking techniques to enhance online safety.

Chapter 67: Multitasking and Food Preparation

Cooking and meal preparation involves multitasking in the kitchen. This chapter provides tips for multitasking while creating delicious meals.

Chapter 68: Multitasking and Crisis Relief

During humanitarian crises, multitasking plays a crucial role in managing aid and relief efforts. This chapter explores multitasking strategies in crisis relief operations.

Chapter 69: Multitasking and Mental Agility

Developing mental agility is key to effective multitasking. This chapter offers exercises and techniques to improve cognitive flexibility and adaptability.

Chapter 70: Multitasking and Sports Training

Multitasking can benefit sports training and performance. We explore how athletes can multitask to enhance their skills and reach peak performance.

Chapter 71: Multitasking and Data Analysis

Data analysts often manage multiple datasets and tasks simultaneously. This chapter provides strategies for multitasking in data analysis and interpretation.

Chapter 72: Multitasking and Personal Finance

Apply multitasking skills to personal finance management. This chapter discusses how to handle multiple financial tasks while ensuring financial stability.

Chapter 73: Multitasking and Academic Research

For researchers, multitasking is essential for managing data collection, analysis, and writing. This chapter offers tips for multitasking during academic research projects.

Chapter 74: Multitasking and Intercultural Communication

Multitasking can enhance intercultural communication and understanding. This chapter explores how to manage cultural cues and communication styles simultaneously.

Chapter 75: Multitasking and Innovation

Innovation often requires handling multiple ideas and projects. This chapter discusses how multitasking can foster a culture of innovation in various fields.

Chapter 76: Multitasking and Personal Productivity

Personal productivity can be optimized through multitasking techniques. We explore how to multitask to accomplish personal goals efficiently.

Chapter 77: Multitasking and Emergency Response

During emergencies, multitasking is critical for emergency responders. This chapter offers insights into multitasking in emergency response scenarios.

Chapter 78: Multitasking and Conflict Avoidance

Multitasking can aid in avoiding conflicts before they escalate. This chapter provides strategies for multitasking to prevent conflicts from arising.

Chapter 79: Multitasking and Business Expansion

Multitasking is vital for business expansion and growth. This chapter discusses how to handle multiple expansion initiatives while maintaining business stability.

Chapter 80: Multitasking and Artistic Creativity

Artists can embrace multitasking to fuel their creative process. We explore how multitasking can inspire artistic expression and innovation.

Chapter 81: Multitasking and Social Skills

Discover how multitasking can improve social skills, such as active listening, empathy, and effective communication in various social settings.

Chapter 82: Multitasking and Disaster Preparedness

Multitasking plays a crucial role in disaster preparedness and response. This chapter provides insights into multitasking during emergency planning and disaster relief efforts.

Chapter 83: Multitasking and Digital Nomadism

For digital nomads, multitasking is essential for managing work, travel arrangements, and personal life while on the go. This chapter offers tips for multitasking as a digital nomad.

Chapter 84: Multitasking and Parenting Styles

Explore how multitasking can be adapted to different parenting styles and family dynamics, ensuring effective parenting while managing various responsibilities.

Chapter 85: Multitasking and Product Development

Innovative product development often involves managing multiple tasks and timelines. This chapter discusses multitasking in product development and launching processes.

Chapter 86: Multitasking and Online Learning Platforms

As online learning platforms become more prevalent, mastering multitasking skills is crucial for students and educators. This chapter provides strategies for multitasking in virtual learning environments.

Chapter 87: Multitasking and Charitable Fundraising

Discover how multitasking can enhance charitable fundraising efforts, managing various fundraising activities while creating a positive impact.

Chapter 88: Multitasking and Emotional Resilience

Emotional resilience is linked to multitasking abilities. This chapter offers insights into managing emotions effectively while multitasking.

Chapter 89: Multitasking and Community Building

Multitasking is valuable in community building and engagement. This chapter provides tips for multitasking while nurturing a strong and cohesive community.

Chapter 90: Multitasking and Supply Chain Management

In supply chain management, multitasking ensures seamless logistics and operations. This chapter discusses multitasking strategies in supply chain processes.

Chapter 91: Multitasking and Interior Design

Interior designers often handle multiple design elements simultaneously. This chapter offers insights into multitasking during interior design projects.

Chapter 92: Multitasking and Mind Mapping

Mind mapping is a powerful multitasking technique for organizing ideas and information. This chapter discusses how to use mind mapping to enhance productivity.

Chapter 93: Multitasking and Business Networking

Networking in business involves multitasking to build professional relationships and expand opportunities. This chapter provides tips for multitasking during networking events.

Chapter 94: Multitasking and Mobile App Development

Mobile app developers often manage multiple aspects of app development concurrently. This chapter explores multitasking in mobile app development processes.

Chapter 95: Multitasking and Cyber Ethics

Multitasking can be applied to uphold ethical standards in cyberspace. This chapter discusses multitasking strategies to promote cyber ethics.

Chapter 96: Multitasking and Academic Conferences

Academic conferences require effective multitasking to manage exhibitions, networking, and learning opportunities. This chapter offers tips for multitasking during academic conferences.

Chapter 97: Multitasking and Environmental Conservation

Multitasking plays a role in environmental preservation efforts. This chapter discusses how to manage multiple conservation initiatives while making a positive impact.

Chapter 98: Multitasking and Effective Communication

Effective communication often involves multitasking, such as managing verbal and nonverbal cues simultaneously. This chapter explores multitasking in communication scenarios.

Chapter 99: Multitasking and Cultural Integration

Multitasking can enhance cultural integration experiences, such as learning a new language while adapting to a different culture. This chapter furnishes insights into cultural multitasking.

Chapter 100: Multitasking and Data Privacy

In the digital age, multitasking is essential to safeguard personal data and maintain privacy. This chapter discusses multitasking strategies for data privacy protection.

Chapter 101: Multitasking and Crisis Counseling

Crisis counselors often handle multiple aspects of counseling simultaneously. This chapter offers insights into multitasking during crisis counseling and intervention.

Chapter 102: Multitasking and E-Commerce Management

E-commerce managers multitask to oversee online stores, inventory, and customer support. This chapter provides tips for multitasking in e-commerce management.

Chapter 103: Multitasking and Conflict Transformation

Conflict transformation requires adept multitasking skills to facilitate constructive dialogue and resolution. This chapter discusses multitasking strategies in conflict transformation efforts.

Chapter 104: Multitasking and Technical Writing

Technical writers multitask to produce clear and extensive documentation. This chapter explores multitasking in technical writing processes.

Chapter 105: Multitasking and Workplace Training

In workplace training, multitasking skills are essential for trainers managing various learning objectives and participants. This chapter offers tips for multitasking in training sessions.

Chapter 106: Multitasking and Time Zones

Managing tasks across different time zones requires effective multitasking and communication. This chapter discusses multitasking strategies for international collaborations.

Chapter 107: Multitasking and Remote Collaboration Tools

Remote collaboration tools aid in multitasking and transmission for virtual teams. This chapter explores the use of such tools to enhance productivity.

Chapter 108: Multitasking and Learning Assessments

Multitasking can optimize learning assessments, such as quizzes and exams. This chapter provides strategies for multitasking during assessment periods.

Chapter 109: Multitasking and Innovation Culture

Multitasking contributes to fostering an innovation culture within organizations. This chapter discusses multitasking's role in promoting creativity and idea generation.

Chapter 110: Multitasking and Cross-Cultural Negotiations

Cross-cultural negotiations involve multitasking to navigate cultural nuances and communication styles. This chapter offers insights into multitasking during international negotiations.

Chapter 111: Multitasking and Digital Storytelling

In digital storytelling, multitasking enhances content creation and audience engagement. This chapter explores multitasking techniques in storytelling platforms.

Chapter 112: Multitasking and Human Resources Management

Human resources managers multitask to handle recruitment, employee relations, and organizational development. This chapter provides tips for multitasking in HR management.

Chapter 113: Multitasking and Real Estate Transactions

Real estate agents multitask to manage property listings, client communications, and negotiations. This chapter discusses multitasking in real estate transactions.

Chapter 114: Multitasking and Health Technology

Healthcare professionals multitask in utilizing technology for patient care and data management. This chapter explores multitasking in health technology integration.

Chapter 115: Multitasking and Inclusive Education

Multitasking in inclusive education ensures equal opportunities and support for all learners. This chapter discusses multitasking strategies for inclusive classrooms.

Chapter 116: Multitasking and User Experience Design

User experience designers multitask to create intuitive and user-friendly interfaces. This chapter explores multitasking in UX design processes.

Chapter 117: Multitasking and Philanthropic Endeavors

Multitasking aids in philanthropic endeavors and charitable activities. This chapter offers insights into multitasking in philanthropy and giving back to the community.

Chapter 118: Multitasking and Environmental Impact Assessment

Environmental impact assessments involve multitasking to analyze ecological and social factors. This chapter discusses multitasking in environmental impact assessment processes.

Chapter 119: Multitasking and Creative Collaboration

Creative collaboration benefits from effective multitasking and idea sharing. This chapter explores multitasking in collaborative artistic projects.

Chapter 120: Multitasking and Social Media Influence

Social media influencers multitask to manage content creation, engagement, and brand collaborations. This chapter provides tips for multitasking as a social media influencer.

Chapter 121: Multitasking and Humanitarian Aid

Humanitarian aid workers multitask to provide relief and support during crises. This chapter discusses multitasking in humanitarian aid efforts.

Chapter 122: Multitasking and Remote Customer Service

Remote customer service representatives multitask to handle inquiries and provide support. This chapter offers insights into multitasking in remote customer service roles.

Chapter 123: Multitasking and Rural Development

Multitasking can support rural development initiatives by managing diverse projects and community engagement efforts. This chapter discusses multitasking in rural development.

Chapter 124: Multitasking and Crisis Simulation

During crisis simulations, multitasking skills are vital for effective response and training. This chapter explores multitasking in crisis simulation exercises.

Chapter 125: Multitasking and Mobile Journalism

Mobile journalists multitask to report, record, and edit content on the go. This chapter discusses multitasking in mobile journalism settings.

Chapter 126: Multitasking and Business Analytics

Business analysts multitask to analyze data, identify trends, and provide insights. This chapter explores multitasking in business analytics.

Chapter 127: Multitasking and Urban Planning

Urban planners multitask to manage city development projects and infrastructure planning. This chapter provides insights into multitasking in urban planning.

Chapter 128: Multitasking and Event Management

Event managers multitask to harmonize logistics, marketing, and attendee experience. This chapter discusses multitasking in event management.

Chapter 129: Multitasking and Energy Conservation

Multitasking can promote energy conservation efforts by managing energy-efficient practices and awareness campaigns. This chapter explores multitasking in energy preservation initiatives.

Chapter 130: Multitasking and Business Negotiation

Business negotiators multitask to analyze data, communicate effectively, and strategize during negotiations. This chapter discusses multitasking in business negotiation scenarios.

Chapter 131: Multitasking and Corporate Training

Corporate trainers multitask to deliver content, engage participants, and assess learning outcomes. This chapter furnishes tips for multitasking in corporate training sessions.

Chapter 132: Multitasking and Civic Engagement

Multitasking supports civic engagement efforts, such as managing community outreach and advocacy campaigns. This chapter explores multitasking in civic engagement.

Chapter 133: Multitasking and Web Development

Web developers multitask to design, code, and test websites and applications. This chapter discusses multitasking in web development projects.

Chapter 134: Multitasking and Remote Project Collaboration

Remote project teams rely on multitasking to harmonize tasks and communication. This chapter offers insights into multitasking in remote project collaboration.

Chapter 135: Multitasking and Data Visualization

Data visualization professionals multitask to create compelling visual manifestations of data. This chapter explores multitasking in data visualization projects.

Chapter 136: Multitasking and Sustainability Reporting

Sustainability reports involve multitasking to evaluate and communicate environmental and social impact. This chapter discusses multitasking in sustainability reporting.

Chapter 137: Multitasking and Cultural Events Management

Artistic event managers multitask to organize performances, logistics, and audience engagement. This chapter provides tips for multitasking in cultural events management.

Chapter 138: Multitasking and E-Learning Design

E-learning designers multitask to create committing online courses and content. This chapter discusses multitasking in e-learning design processes.

Chapter 139: Multitasking and Humanitarian Engineering

Humanitarian engineers multitask to formulate solutions for communities in need. This chapter explores multitasking in humanitarian engineering projects.

Chapter 140: Multitasking and Virtual Reality Experiences

Virtual reality creators multitask to design, program, and test immersive knowledge. This chapter discusses multitasking in virtual reality development.

Chapter 141: Multitasking and Social Impact Investing

Social impact investors multitask to manage diverse acquisition portfolios and assess social outcomes. This chapter provides insights into multitasking in impact investing.

Chapter 142: Multitasking and Accessibility Design

Accessibility designers multitask to create inclusive products and environments. This chapter explores multitasking in accessibility design processes.

Chapter 143: Multitasking and Medical Research

Medical researchers multitask to conduct studies, analyze data, and publish findings. This chapter discusses multitasking in medical research endeavors.

Chapter 144: Multitasking and Language Interpretation

Language interpreters multitask to provide real-time language translation during interactions. This chapter explores multitasking in language interpretation.

Chapter 145: Multitasking and Mental Health Support

Mental health support professionals multitask to provide counseling and support services. This chapter examines multitasking in mental health care.

Chapter 146: Multitasking and Fashion Design

Fashion designers multitask to create collections, manage production, and supervise presentations. This chapter provides insights into multitasking in fashion design.

Chapter 147: Multitasking and Disaster Recovery

Disaster recovery teams multitask to coordinate relief efforts and reconstruct affected communities. This chapter discusses multitasking in disaster recovery processes.

Chapter 148: Multitasking and Video Game Development

Video game innovators multitask to design, program, and test games. This chapter examines multitasking in video game development projects.

Chapter 149: Multitasking and Corporate Social Innovation

Multitasking supports corporate social innovation initiatives by organizing social effect projects and stakeholder engagement. This chapter discusses multitasking in corporate social innovation.

Chapter 150: Multitasking and Continuous Adaptation

In a rapidly changing world, multitasking facilitates continuous transformation and learning. This chapter discusses the significance of multitasking for staying agile and relevant.

Printed in Great Britain
by Amazon

39849415R00031